THIS BOOK BELONGS TO

COLORING TEST PAGE

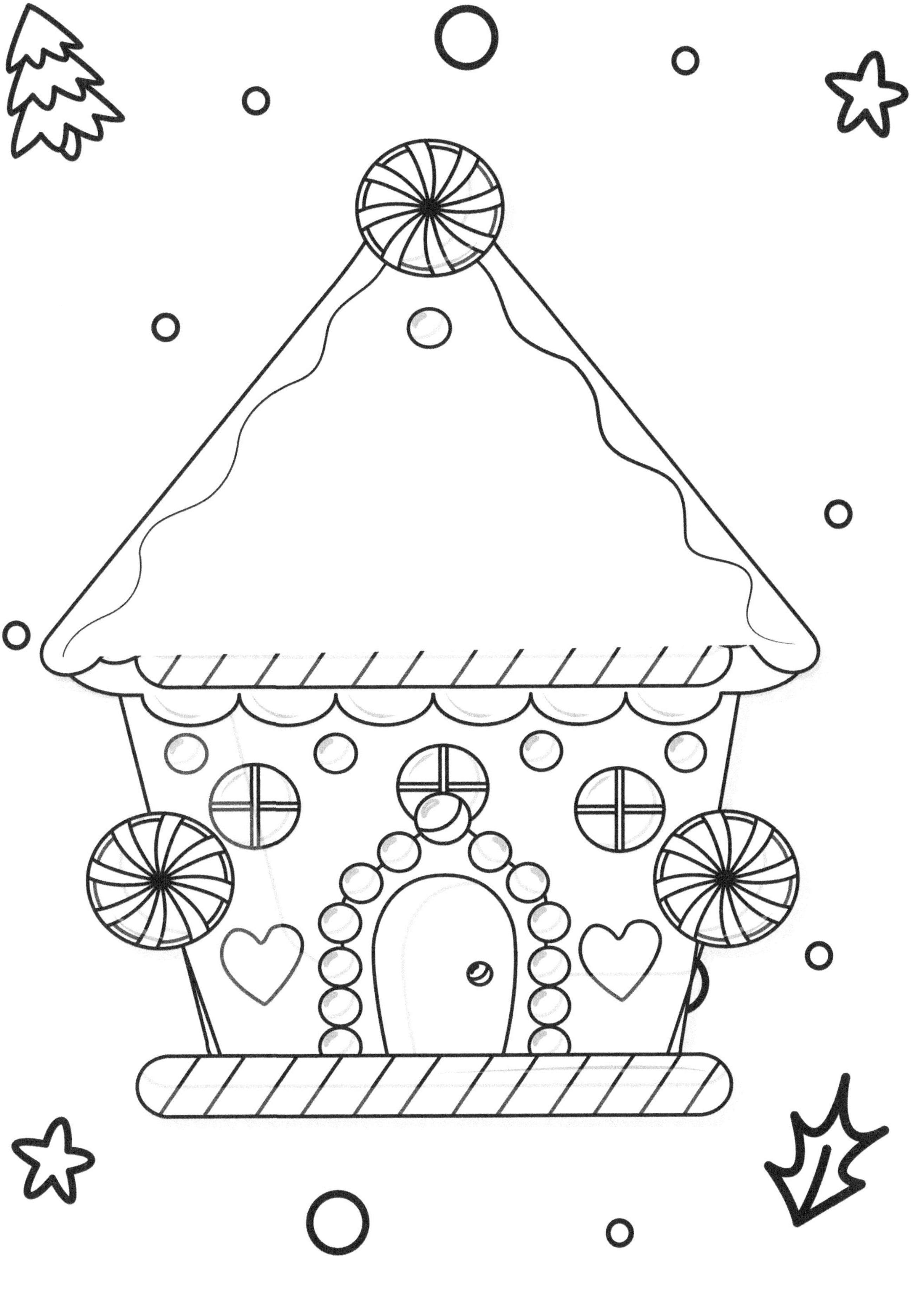

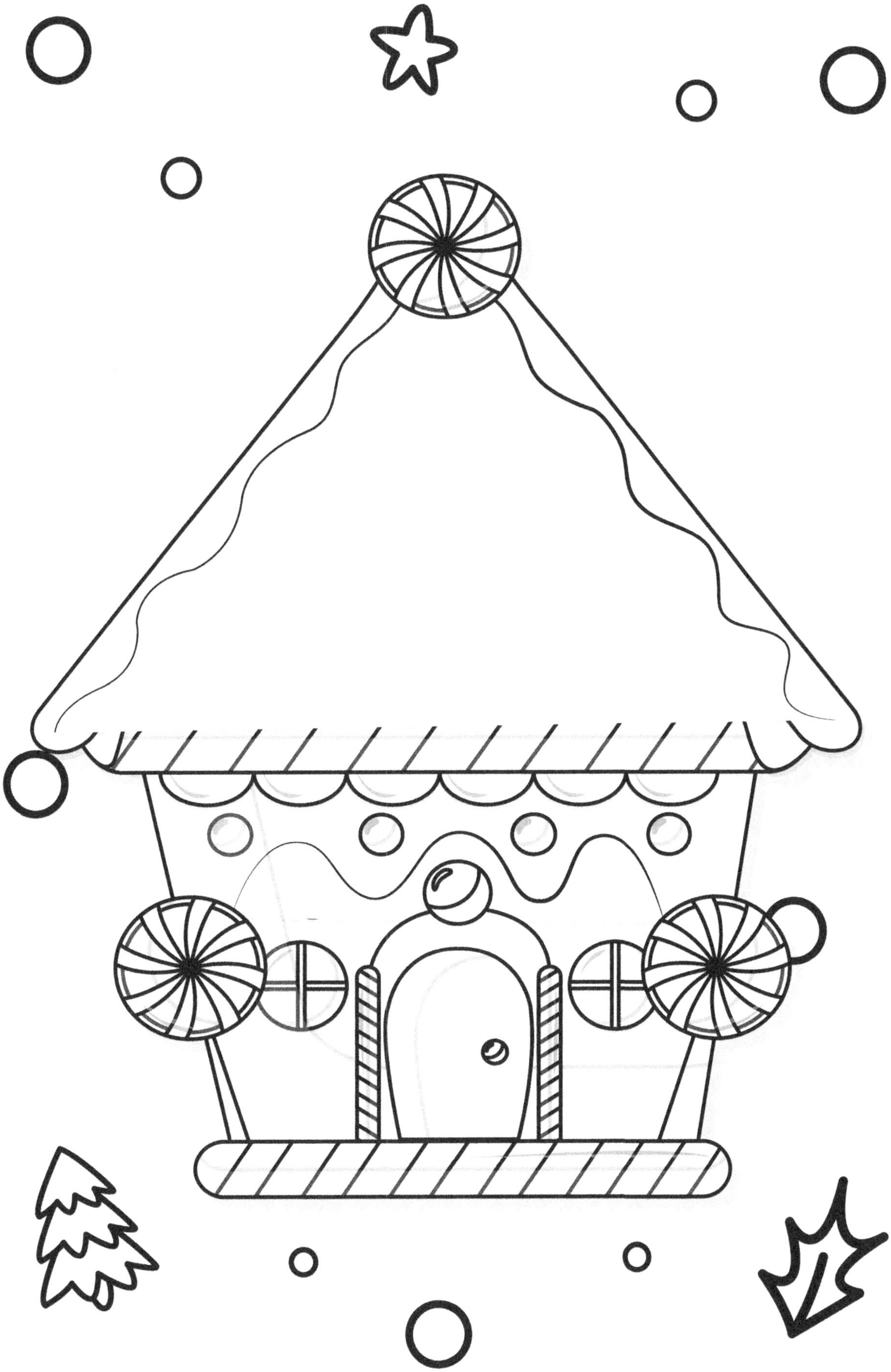

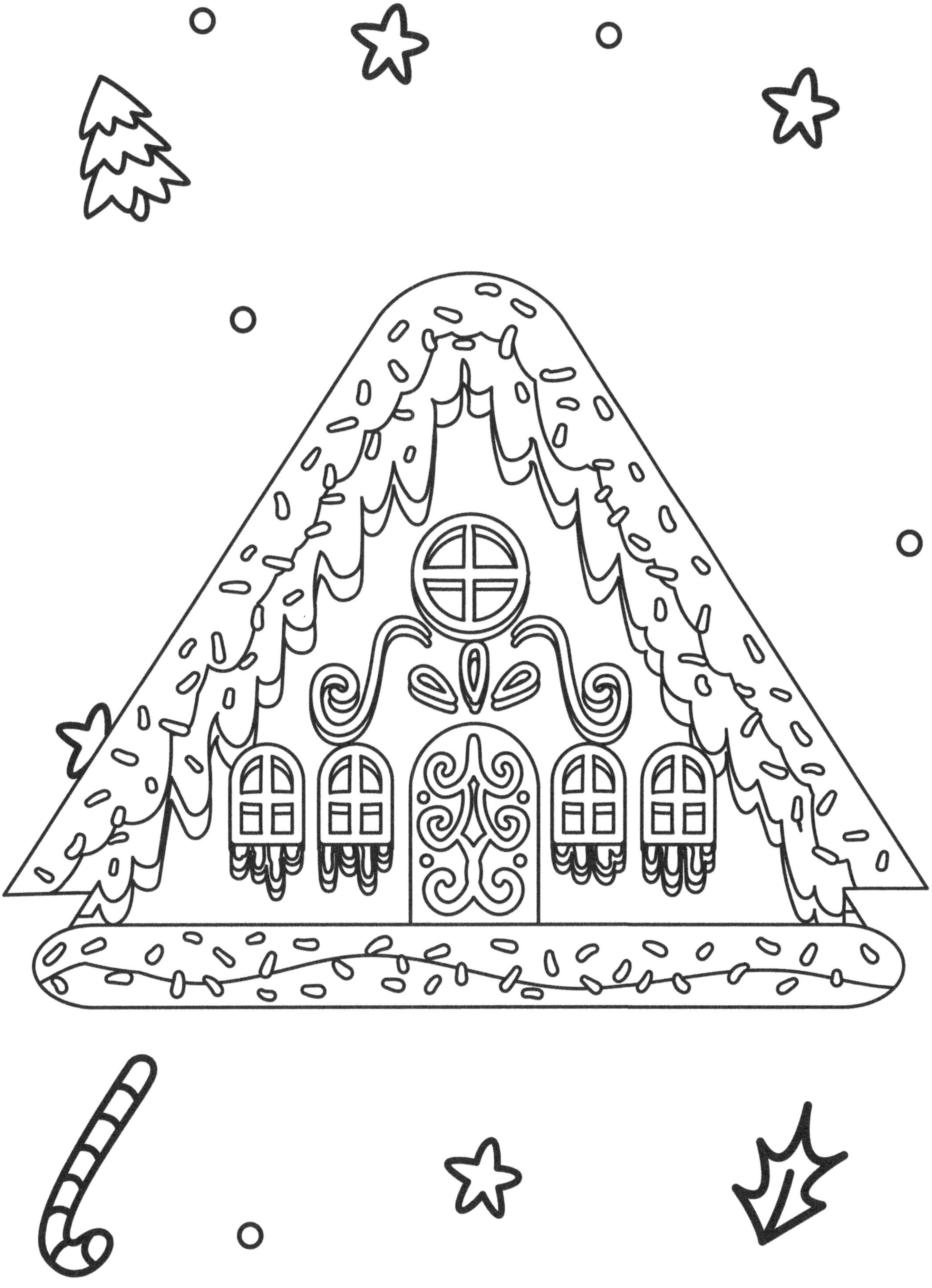

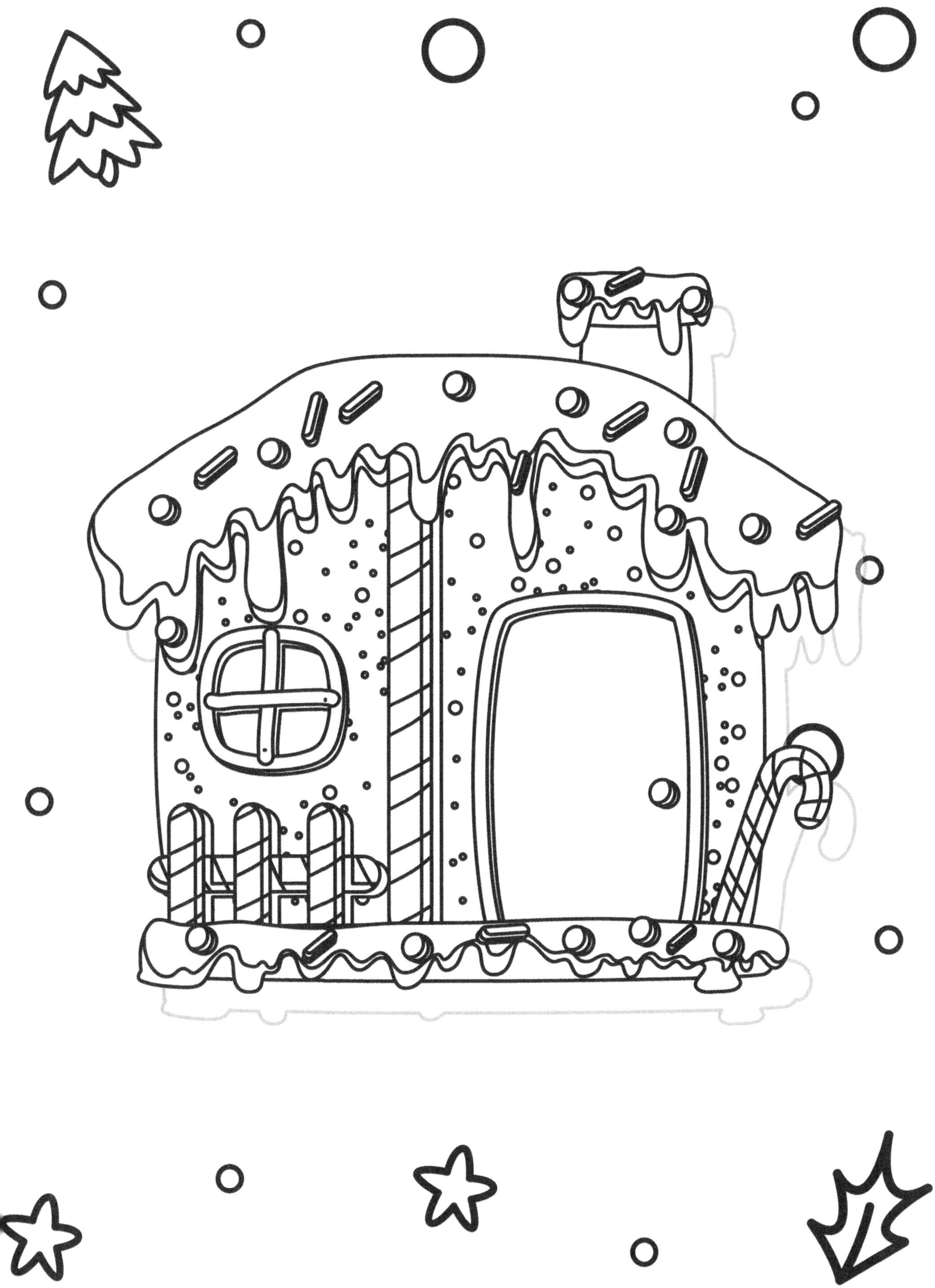

Happy Santa

I'm Coming

Merry Christmas

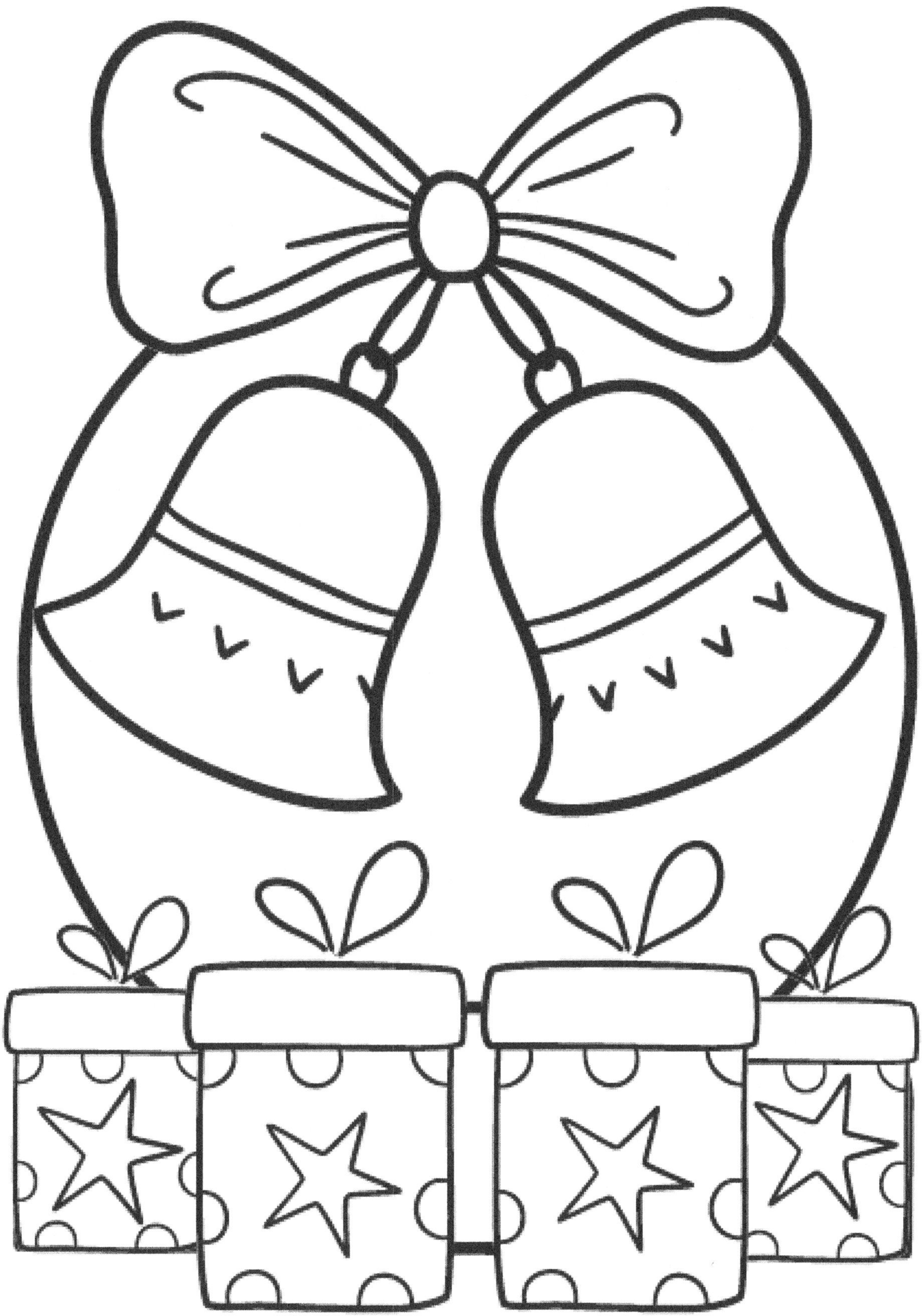

Wish you a
MERRY
CHRISTMAS!